Google Classroom:
The Ultimate Guide To Take Your Classroom Digital

Larry Parris

Copyright © 2017 Larry Parris

All rights reserved.

ISBN: 1974281752
ISBN-13: 978-1974281756

CONTENTS

Introduction iv

Chapter 1 – Advantages of a Digital Classroom 1

Chapter 2 – Adding Students..6

Chapter 3 – Create a Lesson 9

Chapter 4 – Working Across Classes 13

Chapter 5 – Google Forms 15

Chapter 6 – Team Projects 18

Chapter 7 – Reducing Cheating..21

Chapter 8 – Virtual Office Hours 24

Chapter 9 – Personalized Learning...27

Chapter 10 – Classroom for Parents 32

Chapter 11 – Practical Applications 35

Chapter 12 – Special Features 40

Conclusion 44

Thank you very much for getting this book!

I hope, that you will really enjoy reading it. If you want to help me to produce more materials like this, then please leave a positive review on Amazon.

It really does make a difference!

Introduction

More and more schools are moving toward a digital classroom model, if not exclusively then at least for a portion of their interactions with students. These have been available using programs like Blackboard for years. Google's entry into this space, Google Classroom, is one of the most comprehensive digital classroom platforms that's available for any teacher looking to take their class into an online space.

If you're not familiar with this kind of program, you may be a bit confused about exactly what Google Classroom is. The best way to describe it is as a set of productivity tools for teachers that can help you to better organize your classroom. This includes a portal for storing and distributing documents and assignments, as well as for communicating with students, other teachers, and parents. It was designed in collaboration with teachers, too, meaning it has the teacher's perspective at its heart.

There are four different ways to interact with Google Classroom: as an administrator, as a teacher, as a student, and as a parent or guardian. The administrator portal has complete control over all the classes in the school and can view, create, or delete classes, add or remove students and teachers, or view any work being done in any classes.

The teacher and student portals are the ones that will be interacted with most frequently, however. Teachers have the option to create classes and add or remove students or other teachers just like administrators. They can also add assignments and materials to the class stream and interact with students by grading their work, giving them feedback, or communicating with them directly through messages.

The student portal shows them all the work that has been assigned to them, along with any information connected to a class that they have permission to view and any grades or feedback they've been given by the teacher. While parents can't interact with the portal directly, they can receive summaries of their child's work on either a weekly or a daily basis, making it much easier to stay involved in their academic life and know about any big assignments coming up.

The Google Classroom interface has three different sections that you can interact with as an administrator, teacher, or student. The "About" page contains general information about the given class, and is a great place to post a syllabus, give info on tutoring or office hours, or post any links to other sites that will be used throughout the course.

The "Students" page shows the individuals enrolled in the course. The "Stream" is where you'll find assignments, announcements, and other active materials for the class. Each of these three sections will offer different actions and options depending on what kind of account you're using.

Once you've signed up with Google Classroom and chosen your type of account, you can begin to interact with the portal and get a feel for the interface and the tools it offers. While it's incredibly easy to get started with the system, follow the information in this guide as you're going through the program can help you make sure you're not missing any major or useful features of this comprehensive program.

As we get further into the digital age, more and more schools are utilizing technology to help increase student engagement, reduce costs, and maintain better systems. If you're on the fence about employing such technology in your own classroom, taking a moment to learn about Google Classroom's capabilities will likely convince you to give it a try.

Chapter 1 – Advantages of a Digital Classroom

Whenever you're implementing new technology, it's important to ask yourself what function it will serve and whether it will improve the overall environment of your classroom. Many digital classroom interfaces that were released in the past could be clunky or difficult to use; teachers sometimes felt they spent more time struggling with the technology than using it to their advantage.

The programming that underpins the digital classrooms of today has improved tremendously since these early implementations. Whether you want to use the interface as a supplement to in-person classes, during in-person classes, or as an entirely online learning environment, the digital classroom can offer several major benefits over the traditional set-up.

Google Classroom specifically has several advantages over the other available options. First of all, it's completely free for both the teachers and the students for any school or registered non-profit. Anyone with a Google account can sign up to be a student or guardian, also at no cost to the user.

It is also significantly easier to get started with Google Classroom than it was with past iterations. It is easy for both teachers and administrators to add students and manage classes. Once your class is set up, you can make announcements, post assignments, or submit grades with a simple click.

Because it is a Google product, Classroom works seamlessly with other programs like Google Docs, Google Drive, Google Forms, and Google Calendar. This greatly expands your options for how you interact with your students using programs you're all already familiar with.

Google is also very conscious as a company about internet security. They do not use any information from Google Classroom for advertising purposes, and make sure it's completely secure so no one else can, either. This protects the privacy of both students and teachers who use the interface.

Digital classrooms in general also have some distinct advantages over traditional set-ups. If you're still not sure how Google Classroom could be useful for you, reading through some of the ways it can be helpful for teachers may just sway you toward giving it a try.

Save time

In a traditional classroom, assigning work meant printing copies for the entire class and distributing them manually. This might not be so much work for a single-page assignment, but any kind of significant assignment could take a lot of time to prepare. The teacher also had to keep track of students who weren't in class that day and how to get the work to them, as well as planning reminders for large projects and conveying assignment information to interested parents.

The digital classroom puts all these actions in one place. Rather than print off an assignment, you can simply post a new assignment to the class stream; students can work on it and submit it directly in the portal. Announcements, due date reminders, and extra materials all go through this one interface. You can even easily re-use assignments from past classes, saving you lots of time in digging through old files.

Grading is also much easier on a digital classroom. For simple quizzes, you can set up a Google Form to automatically grade multiple choice style tests. For more in-depth assignments, it is much easier to click through files in a drive than to shuffle a giant stack of papers. Entering grades is also quick and easy through the interface. Since the information is communicated to students in real time, you're saving their time, as well, with no more waiting until the next class for a grade on an assignment.

Stay organized

Each class you're teaching or taking on Google Classroom has its own easy-to-find interface. Assignments, announcements, and other information are automatically sorted in the stream, and are saved into a Google Drive folder with the same name as the class header. The entire interface is searchable, too, if you're having trouble finding what you're looking for.

Using your Google Calendar to stay organized!

By using Classroom in conjunction with Google Calendar, your students can see all their assignment due dates in one place, so they'll be less likely to forget—and since the assignment is saved on a drive instead of shoved in their backpacks, they won't be able to lose it.

Teachers will find it easier to stay organized, as well. You can archive old classes instead of deleting them so that you can continue to re-use the assignments from these courses without having to save extensive paper files. Student grades are also archived and searchable, and you can see at a glance who's turned in their work and who hasn't.

Be more green

If a class of 30 students does one worksheet per day, that's 150 pieces of paper per week—and many of the materials and assignments teachers give out are much larger than a page. Less printing means less wasted paper. Aside from the potential benefit to the school's budget, this also makes digital classroom better for the environment by using fewer resources.

Communicate better (and faster)

Grades and comments are transmitted instantly from teacher to student. Students can also comment and reply on this feedback, allowing for true conversations about student work that encourage deeper learning. It is also much easier to make class-wide announcements and be sure that every student got them. The guardian email summary option also keeps the lines of communication open with parents.

Chapter 2 – Adding Students

There are two different ways you can add students to a specific class on Google Classrooms. Both of them are usable by either teachers or administrators. You can either invite specific students or give them a code they can use to add themselves. If you use Google Groups, you can also invite a group of students at the same time.

To invite students, go to classroom.google.com, and click on the class you want to add to. Click "Students," then the "Invite Students" option at the top. Enter a student email address, then click "add recipient." You can do this for multiple students at once, if you'd like. When you're done adding emails, click "Invite."

The class list will update automatically to show the names of all students who have been invited. An email will be sent to the addresses you provided. Before they're officially a member of the class, they'll have to log in to the Google Classroom interface and click "Join" on the class card.

If you meet in person as well as digitally, you may find it easier to simply write the code for the class on the blackboard for students to copy down and enter themselves than to try and collect everyone's email address. In this case, instruct students to navigate to Google Classroom, click

"Add" on the home page, then click "Join Class" and enter the code they've been given.

If your students have trouble using the code, teachers can reset it easily by going into the class in question then clicking on "Students." You'll see the code on the left-hand side of the screen. Click it, and you'll see a "Reset" option. You can also disable the code here if you've finished a course or don't want to allow new students to join. If you change your mind, it can be re-enabled easily using the same process.

Once you've added the students, it's a good idea to post an announcement just to say hello, encouraging the students to post their own greetings. This can get everyone in the mindset of utilizing the interface to communicate. Your students may also be excited to be communicating with classmates online, especially younger students who have never encountered digital classrooms before.

Class size limits

This will not be an issue for the majority of classrooms because the limits Google sets on class sizes are very high, but they're not infinite. You're allowed a maximum of 1,000 users for each class, up to 20 of which can be teachers. Users who log on through a personal Google account may also find there are some restrictions on activity, like how many classes you can create and how many students you can invite; you may want to look into those before you start if this applies to you.

Chapter 3 – Create a Lesson

When you teach using Google Classroom, your assignments become so much more than simply worksheets and projects. The ability to directly attach supplemental materials, videos, links, or other information lets you create comprehensive lessons and share them easily with your students.

To create an assignment, go into the class stream. Hover over the "Add" button at the bottom, then click "Create Assignment." You'll be prompted to enter a title and description or instructions. Whatever you title the assignment will also be the name of the associated Google Drive folder, so make sure it's something you'll be able to easily find. Numbering your assignments can sometimes be a good idea.

You have a lot of options when you create an assignment. You can have it post immediately, save it as a draft, or finish it and schedule it to post at a later date. To post it immediately, click "Assign." For other options, click the down arrow beside it. Your scheduled posts and drafts will be in the "Saved posts" menu. You can choose the due date or set it to have no due date, if you prefer. If you want to get very specific, you can even set the due date for a particular time.

You can also choose whether you assign it to an entire class or just to select students, which makes it easy to give out make-up work or follow-up revisions. The default will be to post to the entire class; to change this, click the down arrow next to "All students" then de-select the option. You'll now be able to choose which students receive the assignment.

Adding links or materials to your assignment is also easy. To upload a file, simply click "Attach" then select the correct file. You can add files both from your computer and from a Google Drive. If you want to remove the attachment, just click the "X." You can also attach links to videos or webpages that students should use as references.

When you upload a file, you'll have three options of how students can interact with it: view only, edit, or create copy. The first is best for reading assignments and other materials the students should reference but not change. The last is best for worksheets and other assignments that students will fill out and post online, letting each student interact with his or her own assignment without impacting anyone else. The middle option is great for collaborative projects, and is very helpful for group or team projects, as will be described later in the book.

You can edit an assignment at any time by clicking on the three-dot "More" menu, then "Edit." Make your changes and save it as you would in any document. Keep in mind that if you've posted the same assignment to multiple classes, editing it will only affect a single class, not every assignment in every class.

After you've assigned the lesson, you can see how the students are interacting with it by clicking on the class, then on the assignment in question. The "Student Work" page lets you review how many students have completed the work at a glance, and determine who still needs to turn in their project. You can also see who you've given feedback to, and view both the work and all comments on it by clicking on the student's name.

When you're interacting with students on an announcement or group-wide assignment, you can add either class comments or private comments for a single student. To make the comment private, click on the student's name; to comment to the whole class, click "Instructions" then "Add class comment."

The student view of all this will look different than what the teacher sees, of course. On their class stream, the assignment will have an "Open" button that will allow them to retrieve and then turn in the assignment. You may find it helpful to include instructions on how to interact with assignments in the class stream on the class' About page, especially for students who have limited experience with digital classrooms.

Grading

Once the student has turned in work, it's time for the teacher to assess it and give feedback. Open the class, then the assignment. There will be a thumbnail for any file that's been attached by a student; click this to open and review the file. When you've reviewed it, you'll see a button that says "Add Grade" next to the student's name; click this and enter their score.

The default point value of any given assignment is 100, but you can change this easily by clicking on "point value" in the assignment page. The system currently only supports whole numbers. This means you can't use decimal points, and you also can't use a letter system.

One of the most helpful things about the digital classroom is that it lets you easily add in comments to explain the grading, correct errors, or point out areas the student should pay attention to. You can use the simple keyboard shortcut Ctrl+Alt+M to add a comment to the student's work at any time.

Chapter 4 – Working Across Classes

If you teach multiple classes within your school, you know it can be tricky to stay organized and maintain accurate records for all of your courses. If you teach the same course semester after semester, maintaining accurate records of the assignments given and how they were received by students can be equally difficult.

By keeping all of your records in one place, Google Classroom gives you a searchable and organized hub for accessing all of your classes, both present and past. They also give you tools that make it easier to re-use announcements, assignments, and other documents across courses.

If you want to post the same assignment or announcement to multiple classes at the same time, click the down arrow next to where it says "For" on the assignment and select all the classes you want it to post to. If you choose this option, you won't be able to select individual students within each class; posts to multiple classes are automatically shared with all students in the class.

You can also easily re-use announcements and assignments you made in past versions of the class. Go into the interface for the current class and hover over the "Add" button. Select the option "Reuse Post." You can then click the class where the original post was published and find the post you want to reuse. It will default to all students, but provided you're only sharing it with a single class, you can select individual students if you'd prefer.

Remember that once you've posted an announcement or assignment across multiple classes edits made to one will not affect the global assignment. You can think of it as the assignment being copied to each class, creating a unique version of the post each time it's replicated.

Re-using old posts and posting to multiple classes at once can be a huge time saver for the busy teacher. This can be especially helpful for setting up cross-disciplinary collaboration or events. You'll also likely find it helpful for more generalized announcements like welcome messages, reminders about upcoming standardized tests, or other information all of your students will need to know.

Chapter 5 – Google Forms

Most of us are familiar with Google tools like Drive and Docs, but those aren't the only free tools the company has that can be handy for teachers. If you're not familiar with Google Forms, you might be surprised by all the ways you can utilize them in your classroom to encourage collaboration, gather information about your students, and speed up your assessment process.

It is much easier to use Google Forms with Classroom than it used to be. When you make a post, you can attach a form using the Google Drive option. Students you share the post with will be automatically linked to a live version of the form. The teacher interface will also offer a link to view the results of the form in a convenient Google Sheet.

You'll need to create your form first before you make the post on Classroom. You can do this straight through Google Drive by clicking on the "New" button, then choosing the three dot "More" menu and looking for Form. To navigate directly, you can instead go to forms.google.com. When you create a form, you have the option of using either multiple choice or open-ended answer formats. Enter your questions and save it, then navigate back to the Classroom interface.

You'll be able to link to the form you've created in the attachments option, under the "Google Drive" icon. Unlike other attachments, you won't be able to view or edit the form directly in classroom. After the form is posted, clicking on it will open the editing screen for teachers, while it will open the form to be filled out for students.

Once a student has filled out the form, it will be marked as done in their assignment list automatically if the form is the only file in the assignment. If there are also other documents or links, the student will need to manually mark the assignment as finished by clicking in the lower right corner.

As students answer the quiz, teachers will be able to see all of their answers in one place on a searchable and sortable spreadsheet. You can then filter the results to see one student's answers, or all the students' answers to a particular question, giving you easier and deeper insight into the results.

Form quizzes

When you set up a Google Form, you have the option of including an answer key along with the questions. This means you can set up quizzes that grade themselves, giving students instant feedback as to their results and saving teachers a lot of mindless work grading stacks of paper tests.

To turn on the answer key, go to the Settings menu (the cog icon) while you're editing your form. The "Quizzes" tab is where you'll be able to turn the option on. You'll only be able to use this tool with multiple choice quizzes, so it's best as a tool with simple assessment of things like vocabulary terms or basic equations.

Chapter 6 – Team Projects

One of the most exciting things about a digital classroom is the extent to which it encourages communication and collaboration, both within the class and between teachers and students in other disciplines. Organizing group and team projects is one area where Google Classroom excels over past digital classroom options.

If you're looking to encourage more collaboration from your class in general, one easy thing you can do is select the middle options when you upload class documents and assignments. This choice makes it so that students can edit the file in question collectively, all at the same time. This works well for spreadsheets and slides, though it may be a bit overwhelming with text-based documents; those tend to function best when edited by no more than five people at a time.

For small group work, you can post the assignment only to the students within a given group, allowing them to work together remotely without interference from other classmates. You could also assign students to a particular group and then title each file clearly so they know which one they're working on. This leaves you the option of allowing the students to sign up for their own groups using an associated spreadsheet. Because the teacher will also be able to see who was interacting with the shared document and for how long, it is easier to identify which team members weren't pulling their weight.

One question you'll have to answer when you're using Google Classroom for team projects is how to determine who will be responsible for submitting the final work at the conclusion of the project. If the online portal is accompanied by an in-class presentation, this may be a moot point. If the final work will be submitted online, though, it may be helpful to designate one team leader who will make sure the group's files are submitted on time.

Google Slides

Another less-used offering in Google's educational arsenal are Google Slides. They work especially well in a digital classroom. Like with the forms mentioned before, you'll have to create the document in the Google Drive interface before you post it to Classroom in an assignment; make sure to post it so that students can edit.

For a whole-class collaboration, you can assign each student their own slide within the document, encouraging them to do their work or post their work to it regularly. This can be a forum where everyone can see and comment on each other's work, encouraging peer to peer feedback and interaction.

Google Hangout

One of the problems with past versions of the digital classroom was that remote communication happened exclusively with text-based messages back and forth. Even the addition of audio to this through Skype or a similar program doesn't generate the same kind of collaborative energy as students will have when engaging face to face.

Setting up a chat room for each group in Google Hangout gives them the option of unsupervised video chat time outside of class. This lets them interact in a more natural way without having to organize a meeting place. This doesn't have to be only for group projects, either; an open-ended Google Hangout associated with the class can be a great way to encourage students to help each other with difficult assignments or projects.

Chapter 7 – Reducing Cheating

One of the main fears most people have about a digital classroom is how to verify that the right person is on the other end of the keyboard—and that they're not looking at someone else's answers while they're entering their own. There are some new features built into Google Classroom to make cheating less likely than it was in similar software of the past, but there are also a few steps that teachers can take to make sure students are doing their own work.

The way Google Classroom saves files in the drives prevents students from seeing each other's assignments. Only teachers and administrators have access to the classroom assignment folder on the Google Drive. This is already an improvement over digital classrooms that use a shared drive accessible by all students, where anyone could look at any copy another student's work if they so choose.

The revision history on the assignment document can also be a handy tool when you think someone may have copied the work of another. You can see whether material was typed, or whether large blocks of text were copied into the interface. You can also see how many times the student accessed and edited the file.

Technology does give students a new variety of ways to cheat, and a lot of teachers feel like having a remote portal for the classroom makes it easier for them to do so. The opposite can be the case if you use the technology wisely, however. When it comes to take-home work, having the assignment online lets the teacher see more information about how the student spent their time working on it.

There are also ways that you can alter your assessment process that can discourage cheating. It is easier to cheat on simple answers, like multiple choice, single word, or true/false responses. Students will be forced to do their own work if you ask more open-ended questions that demand higher-level thinking.

This doesn't mean you can't use simpler questions in the course of your assessment, but you can remove the motivation to cheat by omitting those scores from a student's final grade. The assessment in this case becomes purely informative, giving you and a student a sense of how well they're grasping the material. There is no motivation to cheat in this scenario; it would only keep them from learning the skills they would require to perform their graded tasks well.

Because work can be turned in and returned to the student as many times as you'd like, you can also create multiple checkpoints where the student turns in their work so far during the course of working on an assignment. This forces the student to do the work incrementally, decreasing their need to cheat as they're rushing to finish an assignment last minute.

Chapter 8 – Virtual Office Hours

Office hours can be a great opportunity to interact with your students one-on-one. For some students, it can be a chance to get some personalized tutoring on topics they're struggling with; for others, it can be a chance to bring up concerns or issues in a private setting. As valuable as they are to the learning process, however, office hours can also be tricky to set up in a physical class room, especially considering the demands that are placed on teachers' time both during and outside the school day.

Using Google Hangout in conjunction with your Google Classroom interface can be a great way to offer your students office hours without having to arrange an in-person meeting. The only demand on the teacher's time is that they be at their computer and available to chat during the times specified. It is also more convenient for the student, who can log in from home rather than staying after school or sacrificing their lunch period.

The easiest way to set up virtual office hours is by utilizing the "About" page of the Classroom interface. You can include a permalink to the class' Google Hangout that will stay active for the entirety of the semester or school year. It's easy for the teacher to set up, and students only have to click this link to open a video conference.

You may even find this arrangement is so easy that you want to use Google Hangout video conferences for other meetings, as well. It can be an easier way to set up parent-teacher conferences, for example, and can be used for both group and individual tutoring sessions. If you decide to go this route, you can change the settings in your Google Calendar to create a video conference link any time you set up an appointment. Scroll down in the "Settings" menu until you see the line that says "Automatically add video calls to events I create." Select "Yes" and click "Save at the bottom to put this into effect.

Creating a permalink on your Classroom About page to your Google Hangout office hours is just as easy. If you haven't used Google Hangout in the past, your first step will be to install the plug in. You can navigate directly to the Hangout site or click on any event in your Calendar that shows "join video call" as an option.

Open the room that you'll be using for the office hours. At the top of the window, you'll see a URL. This is the "jump in link" that you can send to someone to invite them to join the chat. Copy this link, then go over to your Classroom interface. On the "About" page, you'll see a button that says "Add materials." Click on this, then look for the icon that looks like a chain. Paste the link into the box that opens up here, followed by "Add" and then "Post."

Once you've added the office hours to your page, navigate back to it and double check to make sure the link copied and is functioning correctly. You can also enter a description on this page if you want to specify what kinds of issues the office hours are appropriate for, or any other information that you think students will need to know.

Virtual office hours are one more of the many ways Google Classroom can be used to streamline the educational experience. It is also a telling example of how various different Google apps and programs can be used together to great effect to maximize the value your students get out of your class time.

Chapter 9 – Personalized Learning

When you think about personalization in regards to an app or online program, your mind likely goes straight to the technical components, like the various settings or the appearance of the interface. While you can certainly do this kind of personalization in Google Classroom, as well—and may have some fun playing with different themes and personalized images for the class stream—the personalization of the learning process that you can achieve with Google Classroom is a much more serious and significant topic.

Educators have known for a long time that different people learn in different ways. The structure of the typical classroom necessitates more of a "one size fits all" approach, aimed at doing the most benefit for the largest percentage of the population. While some students will have an ideal learning experience, there will also be outliners on both sides of the spectrum, some students struggling to keep up while others get bored, potentially becoming a distraction.

Using the tools available to you on a platform like Google Classroom can help you to customize the class to suit the needs of all students. It becomes much easier to distribute extra or alternative assignments to select individuals within the class, or to offer extra tutoring or resources for those who are struggling, in a way that doesn't call attention to them in front of the entire class.

Distributing materials through Google Classroom can also save valuable class time, which gives you more time in each meeting to interact with your students. You can upload the syllabus or directions to a project to the class and give them all an assignment to read it before coming to class so you can spend less time talking at them, explaining the class or project. Providing course materials in this way also encourages students to be more independent learners.

Perhaps the most valuable tool for personalized learning that Google Classroom provides is the chance for the teacher to see the student's process. A quick look at the revision history of an assignment can reveal a lot of information. It shows what day and time the student did the work, how long they spent on it, and how many times they stepped away and came back. This can let you identify procrastinators and help them develop better study habits.

Some of the things you learn reviewing information about your students' habits may surprise you. You may discover that some of your best students habitually put off their work to the last minute—a sign, perhaps, that they are not being sufficiently challenged by the material and may benefit from more advanced concepts that push them toward deeper learning. Whatever you discover, getting a better overall picture of the student's learning style can let you more effectively guide their education.

Weekly check-ins

Getting one-on-one time with the teacher can be a rare and valuable thing in a child's education. There are often twenty or more different students vying for the teacher's attention during class; more timid students can easily get lost in the mix. A digital classroom offers you a quick, easy way to interact with all of your students individually.

Weekly check-ins are once a week assignments where each student gets a chance to voice a concern, suggest an idea, or ask a question and get fast, private feedback from the teacher. You can make this a thing that happens during class time or spend one lunch period each week at your computer instead, ready to interact with your students—whatever works best for your classroom environment. This can be very beneficial for the teacher, as well, letting you tweak your future lessons accordingly to be more effective.

You can use a Google Form for the weekly check-in if you find that to be easiest, but that doesn't always give you the best forum for addressing each student's concerns. Setting it up as an assignment copied to each student is usually an easier way to go.

Comments and discussions

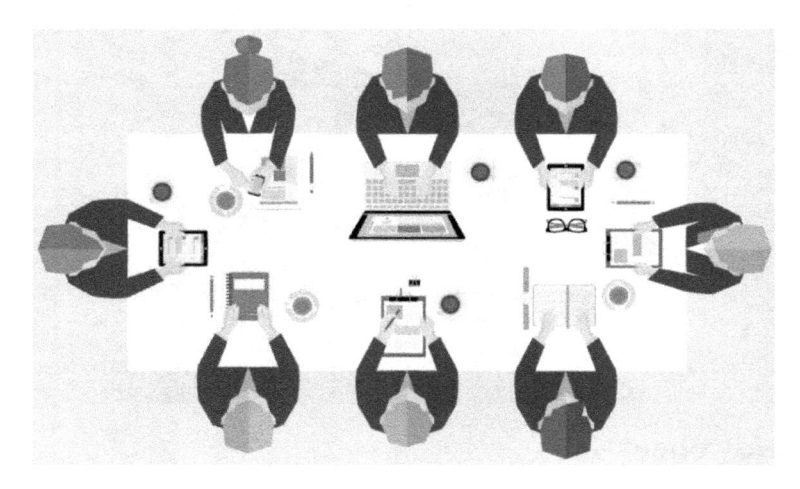

There are various levels of interpersonal interaction that you can engage in on Google Classrooms. One popular choice is to set up an all class discussion and require each student to make at least one post. While you will still end up with some students who are far more loquacious than others, this will at least make sure you're hearing from every student a little bit. It will also make it easier to identify those students who are more reticent and may need some help coming out of their shell.

When you leave a comment on a student's work in Google Classroom, you should think of it less as a static editorial mark and more as the beginning of a conversation. Ask the student questions that will deepen their understanding of the topic, or push their thoughts into an unexpected direction. Encourage students to post comments of their own, pointing out places they didn't feel comfortable with their work or asking for clarification on something they answered incorrectly.

The most important tool for personalizing the learning process is not the digital interface itself but the teacher's ability to interact with it productively. Encouraging them to post comments and engage in online discussions allows you to get a sense of the students' personalities, both online and in person. This knowledge will be instrumental in providing each student with the best learning environment.

Chapter 10 – Classroom for Parents

It can be hard to find ways that parents can become more involved with the educational process. While there are always report cards and parent-teacher conferences to give them a glimpse into their student's academic life, keeping parents in the loop on the student's week to week progress is a responsibility that more often falls to the student himself, for better or worse.

While parents and guardians can't create log-ins to view student work directly on the Google Classroom portal, the email summary feature is an easy way to make sure parents are getting all the information on how their child is performing in school. It makes it easy for the parent to choose his or her own level of involvement, too, and you can synch the system with Google Calendar to add upcoming events and important due dates directly to the calendar.

Inviting a parent or guardian to receive email summaries follows the same process as inviting students to the class. Any administrator or teacher in the class can send the invitation. Simply enter the parent's email address and associate it with their student, then send the invite. The parent will have 120 days to accept the invitation, and will only need to have a Google account of some kind to edit the summary settings; the invitation can be sent to any email address. Once the parent has accepted the invitation, they will receive a confirmation email, as will their student and the person who sent the invitation.

The weekly summary provides a lot of useful information. It will include any missing work that is late and has not been turned in by the time the email is sent. It will also include information on any approaching due dates, along with an overview of the class' activity for the week, like assignments posted, questions recently asked, or announcements that have been made.

Parents can choose to receive the email summary daily or weekly. If they choose daily, the timeframe of upcoming due dates will be limited to those occurring in the next few days. Parents can also unsubscribe from the summaries at any point if they decide they'd rather not receive them.

A quick summary of activity delivered automatically to the parent's inbox is for many teachers the perfect solution for the problem of how to keep parents in the loop on classroom goings on. Parents typically find the reports succinct and easy to interpret, letting them receive information only when it's relevant; if there's no activity to report for a given day or week, no summary will be sent.

Chapter 11 – Practical Applications

By this point, you're probably seeing a whole host of ways that Google Classroom could help you stay organized, save time, and improve the student experience in your school. Even aside from these obvious benefits, however, there are a variety of practical applications and uses for the interface—including those outlined in the sections that follow.

Data collection

Any given course generates a lot of data, both on the teacher's ability to convey the subject and on the student's response to it. Google Classroom makes it easy to collect all of that data into one place, letting you review it and look for weaknesses or patterns you may not have seen before.

The information that is collected by Google Classroom can be easily exported into spreadsheets and graphs to give you a visual representation of the class' progress. All of the assignments, announcements, and materials used for any given class will always be saved in the corresponding folder on the Drive, so you can go back to reference this data at any time.

Refining the curriculum

As an ancillary application to the collection of data, Google Classroom can be used to refine your curriculum. This is true both on a personal, teacher by teacher level, as well as in the broader sense of a school district looking to implement system-wide changes.

On an individual teacher level, the instant student feedback you can receive on Classroom can let you see which of your lessons worked and which ones didn't. You can leave your own comments on assignments that need to be tweaked before they're re-used. You may find it helpful to create a designated folder on Drive for lessons awaiting revision so you can keep them all in one place, and won't accidentally re-assign any of them before they're corrected.

On a broader scale, the data that's collected on Google Classroom is easy to put into a form that can be shared with school boards and other governing bodies to support or oppose proposed changes. It can be difficult to put a tangible face on concepts like student engagement or complex learning in traditional classrooms. A digital classroom gives you more options for isolating and defining these important aspects of the classroom environment in a way non-educators can understand.

Cross-curricular projects

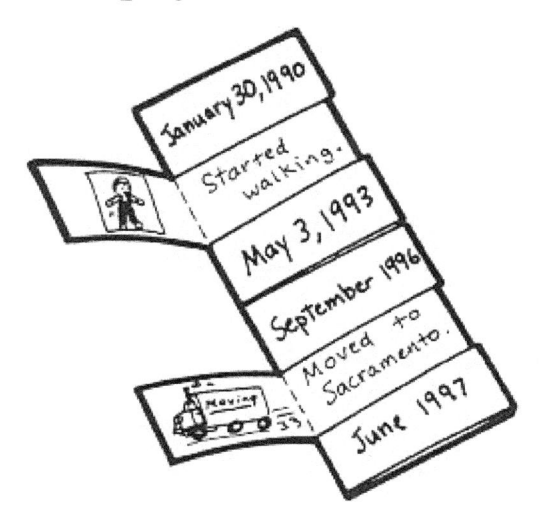

Interdisciplinary learning has been shown to have major benefits for students when they move on to college classrooms and eventual careers, but it can be difficult to work into the traditional structure of the school day. Using a virtual classroom makes it significantly easier to coordinate cross-disciplinary projects.

Up to 20 different co-teachers can be added onto any given class, giving them full access to all projects that are completed within it. You can also share files from the Google Drive with other teachers to easily transfer information about a specific student or project. By working Google Calendar into the process as well, you can easily align deadlines, plan events, and coordinate lessons to encourage deeper shared learning across subject boundaries.

Resource pooling

There are some documents, forms, and supplies that every teacher will need to use at some point during their class. For a long time, the teacher's lounge has been the place where this knowledge is exchanged. Google Classroom makes it even easier to share knowledge and resources with other teachers.

Sending a lesson to another teacher is as simple as locating the class in your Classroom portal and sending them all the materials in the assignment's folder; the resources, materials, and completed assignments will all be stored in the same place, and you can pick out which ones you need.

It is also much easier to integrate mentors, tutors, and educational aides into the learning process using a program like Google Classroom. Tutors can participate in Google Hangout conferences, for example, and can be given access to the calendar or email summaries so they know when important due dates and test dates are coming up.

If there are organized tutoring groups in your school, you could create "by need" classes for these groups and invite the students participating in the program, letting them benefit from the organizational advantages of the interface. You could even do this for peer-based tutoring groups. This drive toward integration is one of the key advantages of a digital classroom space.

Chapter 12 – Special Features

The information about the various aspects of Google Classroom and what you are able to do with them that was given so far in this book will be applicable to the majority of users. You'll be able to start using the interface based on that information, but there are other features and skills within the program that you may not stumble across on your own. A few helpful extra features are described in the sections that follow.

Student portfolios

One interesting feature of Google Classroom is that students are able to create personal portfolios of their favorite work across different class they've taken through the interface. This can be especially helpful when they're applying for scholarships or colleges and need to find relevant samples of their work. If they take classes that use the interface over the course of several years, it can provide them with a picture of their learning history, letting them keep track of learning benchmarks.

Archiving classes

When a class is over, you don't want it sitting on your Classroom home page cluttering up the interface, but you may also want to preserve the class for its data and materials. Archiving a class allows you to shift it off of your active main page without losing all the information.

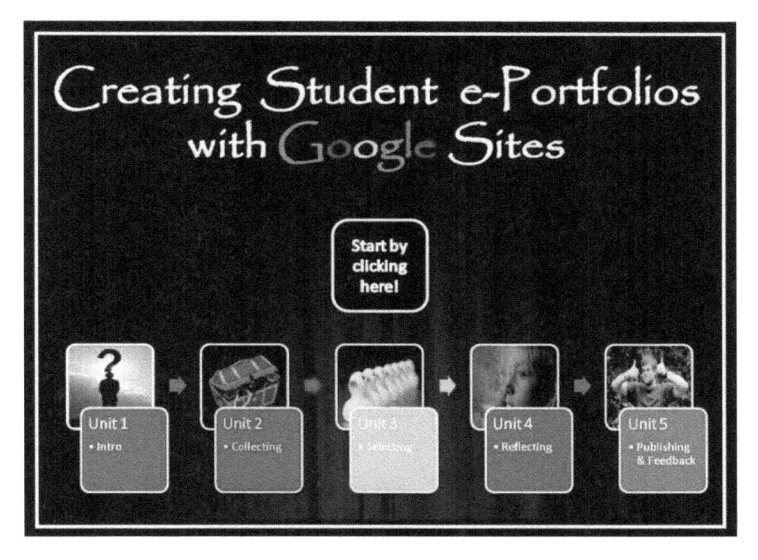

To archive a class, click on the card associated with it and then click the three-dot "More" icon, and look for "Archive" in the menu that pops up. You can restore a class at any time if you change your mind by going through the same steps. Once a class is archived, it's moved to a separate area of the interface, helping you and your students to stay organized and current.

Co-teaching

Most classrooms use a single-teacher format, but there are a variety of reasons you may want to add other teachers onto a course. Google Classroom lets you add up to 20 teachers per class, giving you a lot of different options. If you're working collaboratively with other classes in the school, you could make those instructors co-teachers on your class, as well, so announcements and resources can be shared with everyone who's involved.

The co-teacher function can also be helpful when you're working with tutors and educational aides. It can also be helpful for working with long-term substitutes or student teachers. Regardless of who the teachers are, adding more onto a course can expand the number of people able to grade and respond to student work, and give the students more options of who to contact when they have a question.

Google Classroom

Co-Teacher

Only the primary teacher on the class will be able to delete the class, and cannot be unenrolled or removed from the course. To add other teachers, follow the same steps as for adding students, going to the "About" section at the top of the class card then choosing "Invite teachers." Enter the email of the teacher (or teachers) to be added, then click "Invite." The invited teacher will have to join before they're officially in the class. Once added, teachers have access to

Google Drive folders and can make changes to student profiles and work, the same as the primary teacher.

Muting and deleting

The discussions and comments on the Google Classroom stream are great for encouraging discussion in your class. Just like in a real life classroom, though, there may be individuals who become disruptive, whether because they're bullying other members of the class or simply overloading the conversation with their exuberance.

Thankfully, unlike in real life, on Google Classroom you can mute students to prevent them from talking for a little while. You can mute them for a specific assignment or the entire stream. Students won't see that they've been muted, they simply won't be able to post. Keep in mind that only students can be muted, not teachers.

Teachers can also delete any posts they want to from the class stream if they deem them to be offense or inappropriate. Students can also delete their own posts, but teachers will still be able to see any posts that have been deleted. While the majority of your students won't cause any problems, having these tools available can keep one troublesome student from ruining everyone's experience.

Conclusion

Though they have been around for some time, digital classroom interfaces were of only questionable value for the first few years of their existence. Google Classroom represents a new kind of virtual learning environment, built around ease of use and open communication. The result is a system that is student-centric and greatly beneficial in keeping class materials organized and accessible.

Setting up an account with Google Classroom is free and easy. Set up an account and navigate your way through the various windows to get a feel for how it flows. Even if you're not extremely technically literate, you'll find it to be an intuitively-designed program.

The transition to a digital classroom doesn't have to be all or nothing. You can integrate the aspects of the virtual interface that seem to suit your needs, gradually introducing more technology into your classroom, without sacrificing the in-person atmosphere you've crafted over the years.

Always remember that your Google Classroom interface should be an active, living environment. It will be the most successful when students use it as a resource for collaboration and higher learning, rather than simply a place to take a few quizzes and turn in assignments.

Just like your classroom, the more feedback Google receives about the interface, the better they're able to adjust it to suit the needs of real-life teachers. If you ever notice any features that you think are missing or aren't being utilized to their full potential, send feedback suggesting a change. Google often updates the interface based on user feedback.

The more tools are available to teachers that help them better manage their time and resources, they more energy they're able to devote to actually teaching. If you are a teacher in any capacity, the variety of time-saving tools available on Google Classroom are at the very least worthy of investigation.

I hope, that you really enjoyed reading my book. If you want to help me to produce more materials like this, then **please leave a positive review on Amazon.**

Thanks for buying the book anyway!

I think next books will also be interesting for you:

Windows 10: Complete Beginners Guide To Microsoft WINDOWS 10

LARRY PARRIS

Fire Stick: The Ultimate Guide to your Amazon Fire TV Stick

CPSIA information can be obtained
at www.ICGtesting.com
Printed in the USA
LVHW01s1040100918
589336LV00003B/271/P